Where Animals Live

The World of Owls

Adapted from Jennifer Coldrey's *The Owl in the Tree*

Words by
David Saintsing

Photographs by
Oxford Scientific Films

D1301397

Gareth Stevens Publishing
Milwaukee

Contents

Note: The use of a capital letter for an owl's name means that it is a specific *type* (or species) of owl (such as the Common Screech Owl). The use of a lower case, or small, letter for an owl's name means that it is a member of a larger *group* of owls (such as eagle owls).

Tree-living Owls Around the World

Owls are fascinating birds. There are over 100 *species* of owl in the world. They live among trees in every continent except Antarctica. This screech owl (above left) lives in the jungles of South America. And this little Saw-whet Owl (above right) lives in a pine tree in North America.

Most owls are *nocturnal*. This means that they sleep in the day and hunt at night. Thus owls can be difficult to find. Like this Barn Owl (left), many owls *roost* in tree holes or on branches. The coloring of their feathers helps *camouflage* them while they sit in the trees during the day.

The Size and Shape of Owls

 Most owls have the same basic body shape as this Barred Owl (above left). They sit upright and have a rounded outline.

Owls have large heads, and they seem to have no necks! Owls do have necks, of course — hidden under their thick coat of feathers. Their necks are very flexible and can twist around almost in a full circle. Their bodies remain perfectly still while they do this.

Not all owls are the same size. Some are as big as 2 1/2 feet (75 cm) tall. Others are as small as 4 1/2 inches (12 cm). This Red-chested Owlet from Africa is 6 3/4 inches (17 cm) tall. As *predators*, owls have large *talons* on their feet for catching small *mammals* and birds.

The *plumage* of an owl is usually a mixture of brown and gray. The color can vary, even in the same *habitat* or within the same family.

The Owl's Head and Face

Owls have short, downcurved beaks. This way, its beak does not get in the way of the owl's vision. Owls also have big round eyes which look straight out from a large, flat face. The eyes cannot move, so the owl must turn its head to look in different directions. This is where the "elastic" neck comes in handy!

Unlike most other birds, owls blink by closing their upper eyelids first, as we do. This makes them look almost human!

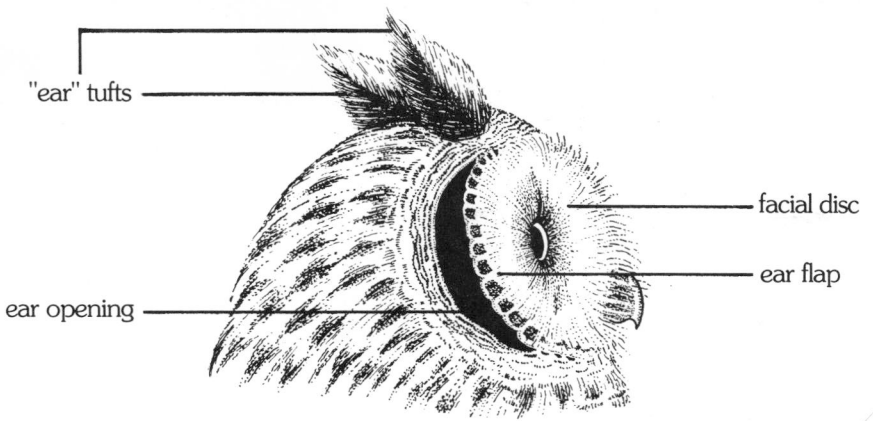

"ear" tufts

facial disc

ear flap

ear opening

The feathers in the owl's face come out from the center to form the "facial disc." Hidden behind these feathers are the owl's ears. One ear is usually larger than the other. This helps the owl locate sounds that might be *prey*. Many owls appear to have ears sticking up from the head. These are not really ears — just tufts of feathers. Owls raise these tufts when they are excited, angry, or scared.

Hunters of the Night

Most owls hunt at night or at dusk or dawn, when the light is poor. Their sharp eyesight and good hearing help them find prey in the dark.

Owls can see better than people at night. But when it is totally dark, owls must use their sense of hearing to detect small animals. It is easy for the owl to turn its head back and forth to locate where a sound is coming from.

Once the owl picks up a noise it turns its head until the sound is equally loud in both ears. This means that the source is straight ahead.

Many scientists believe that woodland owls use their memory to move around the dark at night. These owls hunt over the same area most of their lives, so they get to know their way around. They can thus swoop through the branches without making a sound.

Catching and Killing Prey

Owls usually hunt by using the surprise approach. Once they have located their prey, they can swoop in silently for the kill. The owl's strong legs and sharp talons are very useful for catching and holding a small animal.

Owls' wing feathers are different from other birds'. The front edge of a Barn Owl's wing shows the soft, feathery fringe that helps to silence the sound of the wings striking the air.

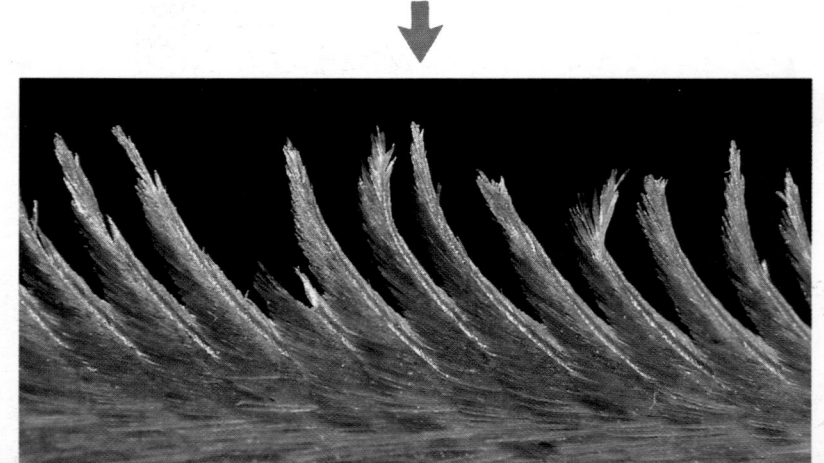

Owls catch most of their prey on the ground. Some owls wait in the trees listening for tiny rustles in the undergrowth. Others hunt while flying low and using their powerful eyes and ears to locate prey.

After killing the prey with its talons and sharp beak, this Saw-whet Owl pauses for a moment before flying off with the prey in its beak.

Food and Feeding

Owls feed on a variety of small animals, ⬆ including mice, frogs, snakes, and insects. This Little Owl brings home an earthworm to its tree hole nest.

Insects are the main food of many small owls, while the large owls catch animals as big as rabbits and squirrels. Large owls also eat other birds, including crows and even smaller owls. There are day-hunting owls in Asia and Africa that can pluck fish right out of the water.

Some owls feed mainly on voles (above) and other small mammals. Owls usually swallow their prey whole. If the owl is eating a bird, it will first remove the feathers.

Many parts of the owl's food cannot be digested. The owl will *regurgitate* these remains in the form of pellets. Look closely at these pellets beneath an owl's roost. The bones, fur, teeth, and other remains will tell you what the owl has eaten!

Courtship and Mating

When mating season comes, the male attracts a mate by hooting loudly. The female answers with a different call. Sometimes, the owls will sing together. Male and female owls are used to living on their own, so they are usually afraid of one another. But the male courts the female to make her less afraid. Many courtship dances, or displays, have not been seen by humans. Only when the female trusts the male will she mate with him.

After they mate, the male and female stay close together. Often they *preen* each other's plumage. They then find a place to lay their eggs. Owls usually do not build much of a nest. Tree-living owls may lay their eggs in the old nest of a woodpecker or squirrel.

Some owls use open nests high in the trees. This owl nest in South Dakota may once have belonged to a hawk or some other bird of prey.

Eggs and Chicks

Owls lay round white eggs. Because the eggs are hidden from view, they do not need to be camouflaged. There are usually three to six eggs to a *clutch*.

The female begins to *incubate* the eggs as soon as the first is laid. This means that the chicks hatch at different times. The first chicks to hatch are bigger and stronger than the rest. If there is not enough food for everyone, the older and stronger chicks are the ones that will survive.

The eggs hatch in 3-5 weeks. The *owlets* are born with their eyes closed. Their mother guards them fiercely and keeps them warm by *brooding* them under her body. The fluffy *down* on this week-old Tawny Owl (above) also helps keep it warm.

These baby Barred Owls wait for their parents to return with food. At first, the mother tears up the food for them. After a few weeks, the owlets can tear up their own food. ⬇

Growing Up

This female Great Horned Owl keeps her *brood* warm in their open nest.

By 3-4 weeks old, most owlets have grown their first real feathers, and they flap their tiny wings to exercise them (near right). Soon they are ready to leave the nest. At first they walk along the branches of the tree, and it is not long before they take their first flight. At this point, however, the young owlets still depend on their parents for food (far right).

After several months, the young owls hunt for themselves. The parents usually must force them out of the nest so they can learn to care for themselves. Many young owls die in their first year because they are poor hunters and cannot find enough food. Others are killed by the cold or by predators. The ones that survive can live from five to 20 years or more.

The Home Life of Owls

Most tree-living owls stay in the same place all of their lives. Each bird has its own *territory* in which it lives and hunts. Territories can cover 40-100 acres (15-40 hectares).

Owls must learn to recognize each other and their boundaries. They do this by calling and displaying to each other. This Barn Owl is defending its breeding territory. It is lowering its wings, thrusting its head out, clicking its tongue, and hissing. ↘

Other owls display their eyes and their "ear" tufts to communicate.

Not all owls stay in their home territory. Some hunt outside their territory and defend it only in the breeding season. Others, like this Great Gray Owl from Canada, must sometimes *migrate* long distances to find food.

Owls mostly like to live alone and come together only to breed. Some, however, do roost in family groups during the winter.

Enemies of Owls

Owls are predators. But they are also the prey of other animals. Snakes and other tree-climbing *carnivores* like this weasel can take eggs or owlets from the nest.

Large owls like this Great Horned Owl also kill and eat other owls.

Other large birds of prey, such as eagles and hawks, will attack owls. Small birds like thrushes, finches, and jays recognize owls as their enemies. They will make a fuss and mob an owl when it is around. And even though they are not really a danger to owls, they can be pests.

One of the greatest dangers to owls is death by hunger and cold during harsh northern winters.

Escape from Danger

Adult owls are safe from most danger on the ground because they can fly away from enemies. Up in the trees the eggs and owlets are safe from animals that cannot climb.

But even in the trees there is some danger in the day to roosting owls. The owls are dozing, and they are not very alert. Thus owls must keep themselves hidden during the day so predators cannot see them.

Roosting owls can usually sleep in peace thanks to their camouflage. As long as this small gray owlet stays still, it will probably not be seen.

Owls can strike out at intruders with their talons. But they rarely attack other animals except for food. They would rather scare their enemies away or escape through the air. Some owls use their large fearsome eyes to scare off mobbing birds or squirrels. They may also raise up their "ear" tufts and puff up their wings. This makes them look much larger than they really are.

Owls and Humans

To the ancient Greeks, the owl was a sign of wisdom. This ancient vase shows Athena, the goddess of wisdom, as an owl. Even today, we often talk of owls as wise old birds. Other people have thought of owls as bringers of bad luck.

Today people are more interested in the real lives of these unusual birds. The scientist to the right is marking an owl to study its behavior.

There are still some people who harm owls. In some countries, owls are hunted for sport or used to attract other birds. These other birds are in turn hunted or trapped for sport.

We sometimes hurt owls by accident with the pesticides we use for our crops. We do even more harm when we cut down trees and destroy owls' habitats. Most countries now have laws which protect owls. In North America, even photographers cannot disturb owls without a license! We can help owls by protecting their woodland homes. Someone built this nesting box (left) for a lucky owl in Norway!

Friends and Neighbors

Owls share their home in the trees with many other birds, including jays, crows, and woodpeckers. This Tawny Frogmouth from Australia is, like the owl, a night hunter. Its huge mouth helps it catch insects in flight.

Bats are also skilled night hunters. This Greater Horseshoe Bat is about to catch a moth in the darkness.

In addition to bats, other tree-living mammals include squirrels, opossums, and, in the *tropics*, even monkeys. These are day hunters. Other animals such as foxes, badgers, and snakes often hunt for prey in the forest. These are night hunters, and they may become rivals of the owl when food is short. Some birds of prey, such as the hawk and the buzzard, are day hunters. Therefore, they do not interfere very much with owls' night-time activity.

Other birds in the owl's habitat build nests which the owl can use. Owls often move into woodpecker holes after the woodpecker leaves.

Life Among the Trees

Most owls feed on small animals that feed on other small animals or plants. The picture below shows that very few animals prey on owls. This means that owls are usually at the top of their food chain. It also means that there must be far fewer owls than prey, or else owls would run out of food and starve to death.

Food Chain

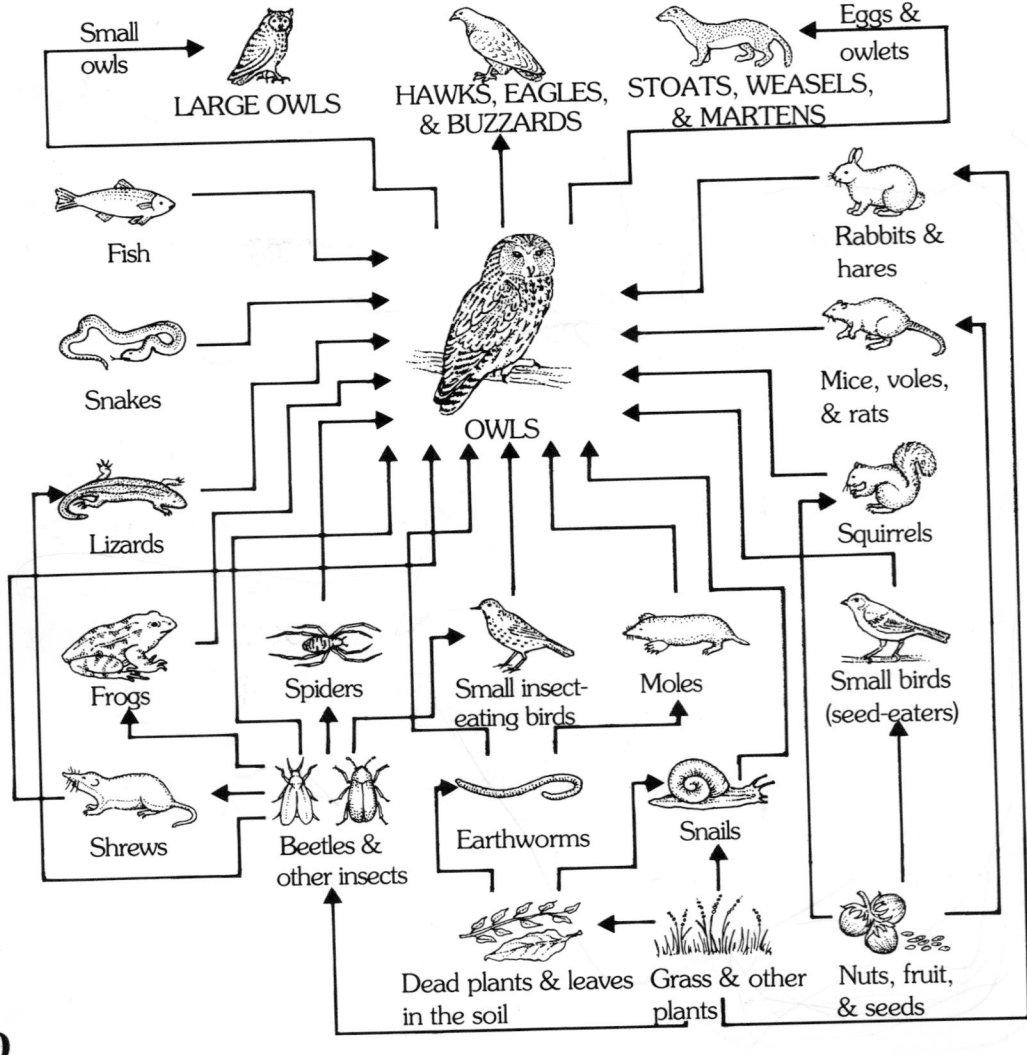

Alert in the darkness, this owl is a skilled night hunter. All owls are well-adapted for their life among the trees, and they have few real rivals in their habitats. Owls play an important part in keeping the balance of nature. People have always been interested in owls, and now we must protect their habitat. Even in the cities, we can help by putting up nest boxes and by planting and saving trees.

Index and New Words About Owls

These new words about owls appear in the text on the pages shown after each definition. Each new word first appears in the text in *italics*, just as it appears here.

Reading level analysis: SPACHE 2.2, FRY 2, FLESCH 99 (very easy), RAYGOR 3, FOG 4, SMOG 3

Library of Congress Cataloging-in-Publication Data
Saintsing, David.
  The world of owls.
  (Where animals live)
  "Adapted from Jennifer Coldrey's The owl in the tree."
  Includes index.
  Summary: Text and photographs describe the lives of owls, including their feeding, breeding, and defense behavior.
  1. Owls--Juvenile literature. [1. Owls] I. Coldrey, Jennifer. The owl in the tree. II. Oxford Scientific Films. III. Title. IV. Series.
QL696.S8S25 1988 598'.97 87-6537
ISBN 1-55532-326-X ISBN 1-55532-301-4 (lib. bdg.)

North American edition first published in 1988 by
Gareth Stevens, Inc.
7221 West Green Tree Road Milwaukee, WI 53223, USA
US edition, this format, copyright © 1988 by Belitha Press Ltd.
Text copyright © 1988 by Gareth Stevens, Inc.

All rights reserved. No part of this book may be reproduced in any form or by any means without permission in writing from Gareth Stevens, Inc. First conceived, designed, and produced by Belitha Press Ltd., London, as **The Owl in the Tree**, with an original text copyright by Oxford Scientific Films. Format copyright by Belitha Press Ltd.

Typeset in Milwaukee by Web Tech, Inc. Printed in Hong Kong by South China Printing Co.
Series Editor: Mark J. Sachner. Art Director: Treld Bicknell.
Design: Naomi Games. Cover Design: Gary Moseley. Line Drawings: Lorna Turpin.
Scientific Consultants: Gwynne Vevers, Graham Martin, and David Saintsing.

The publishers wish to thank the following for permission to reproduce copyright photographs: **Oxford Scientific Films Ltd.** for pp. 4 left, 7, 21 below, and title page (Z. Leszczynski); pp. 10 above, 11, 17 below, 29, and front cover (Ted Levin); pp. 2 and 31 (D.J. Saunders); pp. 3 left, 4 right, and 6 (M.P.L. Fogden); pp. 3 left and 20 (Joe McDonald); pp. 5, 13 above, and 23 (D.H. Thompson); p. 8 (John Gerlach); p. 10 below (G.I. Bernard); p. 13 below (Tim Shepherd); p. 15, 18, 19 left and right (Charles Palek); p. 16 C.M. Perrins); p. 17 above (Philip Sharpe); pp. 20 above and 25 (Breck P. Kent); p. 22 above (Press-Tige Pictures); p. 22 below (Jack Wilburn); p. 24 above (Andrew Lister); p. 24 below (M. Wilding); p. 26 (Stephen Mills); p. 27 (Graham Wren); p. 28 above (J.A.L. Cooke); p. 28 below (Stephen Dalton); Bruce Coleman Ltd. for pp. 9 and 14 (Hans Reinhard); The Louvre Museum, Paris for p. 26.